Our Bill of Rights

Sharing and Re

Mitchell Allen

COMPUTER SCIENCE For the REAL World™

Rosen Classroom™

Published in 2018 by The Rosen Publishing Group, Inc.
29 East 21st Street, New York, NY 10010

Book Design: Jennifer Ryder-Talbot
Editor: Caitie McAneney

Photo Credits: Cover sharpner/Shutterstock.com; p. 4 /Wikimedia Commons; p. 4, 20 (gavel icon) T-Kot/Shutterstock.com; p. 7 (James Madison) AISAEverett/Shutterstock.com; p. 7 Pamela Au/Shutterstock.com; p. 7, 12 (pen and ink icon) ArsenLuben/Shutterstock.com; p. 8 /Wikimedia Commons; p. 8, 16 (newspaper icon) AVIcon/Shutterstock.com; p. 11 wavebreakmedia/Shutterstock.com; p. 11, 15, 19 (megaphone icon) GN ILLUSTRATOR/Shutterstock.com; p. 12 ESB Professional/Shutterstock.com; p. 15 Dragon Images/Shutterstock.com; p. 16 Twin Design/Shutterstock.com; p. 19 Rob Marmion/Shutterstock.com; p. 20 gpointstudio/Shutterstock.com.

Library of Congress Cataloging-in-Publication Data

Names: Allen, Mitchell.
Title: Our Bill of Rights: sharing and reusing / Mitchell Allen.
Description: New York : Rosen Classroom, 2018. | Series: Computer Kids: Powered by Computational Thinking | Includes glossary and index.
Identifiers: LCCN ISBN 9781508137696 (pbk.) | ISBN 9781538324226 (library bound) | ISBN 9781538355367 (6pack) | ISBN 9781538352793 (ebook)
Subjects: LCSH: United States. Constitution. 1st-10th Amendments--Juvenile literature. | Civil rights--United States--History--Juvenile literature. | Constitutional history--United States--Juvenile literature.
Classification: LCC KF4749.A44 2018 | DDC 342.7308'5--dc23

Manufactured in the United States of America

CPSIA Compliance Information: Batch #WS18RC: For Further Information contact Rosen Publishing, New York, New York at 1-800-237-9932

Table of Contents

This artwork shows the signing of the U.S. Constitution in 1787.

The U.S. Constitution

The U.S. Constitution is the **document** that has held the United States together for over 200 years. This document outlines the frame of the U.S. government and promises basic rights to all citizens.

The Constitution separated the government into three branches. One branch makes laws, ones carries out laws, and the other decides if laws are **constitutional**. The Constitution also **declared** which powers went to the federal government and which went to state governments. How was this document created? How can you reuse parts of it in your everyday life?

Creating the Constitution

It took a lot of time and energy for U.S. leaders to write the Constitution. The Constitutional Convention was a series of meetings between government leaders to rework the old ruling document, called the Articles of Confederation.

Constitutional Convention members had to reuse knowledge they'd learned about the Articles of Confederation. What worked? What had gone wrong? Members met from May to September 1787. After that, it took two years for the U.S. Constitution to become law. Next, the Bill of Rights became part of the Constitution.

James Madison wrote the Bill of Rights.

Congrefs OF THE United Stat
begun and held at the City of New-York, on
Wednesday the fourth of March, one thousand seven hundred and eightynin

This is the original Bill of Rights, which became part of the U.S. Constitution in 1791.

What's the Bill of Rights?

The Bill of Rights wasn't added until 1791. James Madison wrote this part of the Constitution to promise basic freedoms to all U.S. citizens.

The first ten amendments, or changes, to the U.S. Constitution make up the Bill of Rights. Today, there are 27 amendments to the Constitution. The Bill of Rights established the rights and rules that cannot be taken away from lawful citizens. This part of the Constitution applies most directly to everyday life. It's often used to make sure all Americans are being treated fairly.

Reusing Rights and Rules

Do you have rights and rules in your classroom? Do you have rights and rules at home or in sports? These are settings where it's important to play by the rules and to speak up for your own basic rights.

Reusing knowledge is one of the best ways to complete a task. It took years and many people to write the U.S. Constitution as we know it. You can reuse the rights and rules they created in other settings. This can save you time and energy. Many amendments can be used in your daily life.

It's important to stand up for your rights in many situations.

You can suggest a classroom rule of **tolerance** towards people of all religions and **cultures**.

Freedom of Religion

The Bill of Rights uses the first amendment to **protect** five basic **liberties**. This amendment affects our lives every day.

The first liberty that's mentioned is the freedom of religion. Some countries around the world control the religions of their people. However, all American citizens have the right to follow any religion. You can practice religion in any way you feel is right. You can reuse this amendment by making it a personal rule to show tolerance to people of all religions and cultures. You can also stand up for your right to your own beliefs.

Freedom of Speech

The second liberty that is protected is the freedom of speech. American citizens are allowed to speak their mind. You can disagree with others and give your opinion without getting in trouble. However, your words should be truthful and fair.

Do you have thoughts or opinions on a certain topic? You might have a favorite football team or a favorite food. You can talk about your thoughts and opinions, as long as it's respectful to others who might have different thoughts or opinions.

Suggest a family rule that everyone can speak their mind, as long as their words are respectful.

Do you have a school newspaper? You can stand up for your right to state true facts and your beliefs.

Freedom of the Press

The press includes newspapers, news television, and other **sources** of news and information. The press is very important because it shares information with U.S. citizens. People who report for the press have the freedom to say what they believe about the government without being punished. However, if they tell lies on purpose, they may be punished.

This freedom is very important. It means that writers and reporters can give facts and the government can't tell them what to write. Next time you read or watch news, you will be benefiting from the free press.

Assembly and Petition

The first amendment also protects the freedom of assembly and the freedom to petition. Freedom of assembly means that citizens are able to join any **political party**, club, or group that they want to. These groups might even peacefully **protest** against a government action.

Freedom to petition means that citizens can tell the government what they want. Citizens may complain about government actions or ask for something to be done. Because of this amendment, you can join groups and clubs, and speak your mind when you think something needs to change.

You can petition your school to take a tougher stand when it comes to bullying.

You can suggest the rules for fair trials when it comes to punishments in your classroom.

Right to a Fair Trial

Several amendments in the Bill of Rights have to do with fair trials and punishments. A trial happens when someone may have done something wrong. A trial decides if a person did or did not commit a crime. Citizens have the right to a fair trial that decides if they broke the law. The government must follow a certain process before jailing a person. The government cannot punish anyone in a **cruel** way.

When someone does something wrong at school or at home, you can make sure they are questioned and punished fairly. You may reuse the saying "innocent until proven guilty."

Reusing Knowledge

Imagine your classroom has to come up with a set of rules and rights. You don't have to start from scratch. You now know a lot about the Bill of Rights and Constitution. The laws contained in this document have been **effective** for hundreds of years, so they must work well.

How can you reuse and share your knowledge of the Bill of Rights to make classroom rules? Think of the situations you come across each day that could benefit from this knowledge. Brainstorm new ways to reuse this historic document!

Glossary

constitutional: Loyal to and following the laws of the U.S. Constitution.

cruel: Causing unjust suffering.

culture: The beliefs and ways of life of a group of people.

declare: To make something known formally.

document: A formal piece of writing.

effective: Producing a desired result.

liberty: The power to do as one pleases; the state of being free.

political party: A group of persons organized for the purpose of directing the policies of a government.

protect: To keep safe.

protest: To strongly oppose something.

source: A supplier of information.

tolerance: Accepting other ideas or points of view.

Index